HOW GLACIERS SHAPED EARTH

by Jane P. Gardner

Ideas for Parents and Teachers

Pogo Books let children practice reading informational text while introducing them to nonfiction features such as headings, labels, sidebars, maps, and diagrams, as well as a table of contents, glossary, and index.

Carefully leveled text with a strong photo match offers early fluent readers the support they need to succeed.

Before Reading

• "Walk" through the book and point out the various nonfiction features. Ask the student what purpose each feature serves.

• Look at the glossary together. Read and discuss the words.

Read the Book

• Have the child read the book independently.

• Invite him or her to list questions that arise from reading.

After Reading

• Discuss the child's questions. Talk about how he or she might find answers to those questions.

• Prompt the child to think more. Ask: What did you know about glaciers before reading this book? What more would you like to learn?

Pogo Books are published by Jump!
5357 Penn Avenue South
Minneapolis, MN 55419
www.jumplibrary.com

Library of Congress Cataloging-in-Publication Data

Names: Gardner, Jane P., author.
Title: How glaciers shaped earth / by Jane P. Gardner.
Description: Minneapolis, MN: 2021.
Series: Earth shapers | Includes index.
Audience: Ages 7-10 years
Identifiers: LCCN 2019028038 (print)
LCCN 2019028039 (ebook)
ISBN 9781645271208 (hardcover)
ISBN 9781645271215 (paperback)
ISBN 9781645271222 (eBook)
Subjects: LCSH: Glaciers–Juvenile literature. Illustrated children's books.
Classification: LCC GB2403.8 .G37 2020 (print)
LCC GB2403.8 (ebook) | DDC 551.31/3–dc23
LC record available at https://lccn.loc.gov/2019028038
LC ebook record available at https://lccn.loc.gov/2019028039

Editor: Jenna Gleisner
Designer: Michelle Sonnek

Photo Credits: David H. Brown/Shutterstock, cover; Santiparp Wattanaporn/Shutterstock, 1; Nicolaj Larsen/Shutterstock, 3; Claus Lunau/Science Source, 4; Wayne Morris/Shutterstock, 5; Denis Burdin/Shutterstock, 6-7; John E Marriott/All Canada Photos/SuperStock, 8; Matt Champlin/Getty, 9; PARADOX_M/Shutterstock, 10-11; David Dennis/Shutterstock, 12-13; pattarastock/Shutterstock, 14-15; Steven Schremp/Shutterstock, 16-17; Laura Pl/Shutterstock, 18; vladsilver/Shutterstock, 19; Gabor Kovacs Photography/Shutterstock, 20-21 (background), 23; Rawpixel.com, 20-21 (boy); Castleski/Shutterstock, 20-21 (sign).

Printed in the United States of America at Corporate Graphics in North Mankato, Minnesota.

TABLE OF CONTENTS

CHAPTER 1
Layers of Ice and Snow...................4

CHAPTER 2
Leaving Their Mark...................8

CHAPTER 3
The Future of Glaciers...................18

ACTIVITIES & TOOLS
Try This!...................22
Glossary...................23
Index...................24
To Learn More...................24

CHAPTER 1

LAYERS OF ICE AND SNOW

The Great Ice Age began about 2.6 million years ago. Thick **continental glaciers** covered much of Earth. Our planet was much colder.

continental glacier

These glaciers are also called **ice sheets**. They spread across huge areas. Most of them melted when the Great Ice Age ended. This was about 12,000 years ago. Today, they still cover Greenland and Antarctica.

Antarctic
ice sheet

Glaciers form when more snow falls in winter than melts in summer. New snow packs down older snow. It turns to ice. The layers of ice and snow pile up.

Glaciers flow, or move, like water. They are heavy and move very slowly. How? **Gravity** pulls them downhill. Jakobshavn Glacier is a fast-moving glacier in Greenland. It moves as much as 150 feet (46 meters) a day!

DID YOU KNOW?

When ice sheets move to the ocean, huge chunks may break off. These become **icebergs**. They float in the ocean. They can sink ships that hit them!

Jakobshavn
Glacier

CHAPTER 2

LEAVING THEIR MARK

Glaciers are so large that they shape the land when they move. How? They break down the ground under them. This makes **till**. They pick it up. As they move, some till is left behind. It can pile up along the edges of glaciers.

till

Ponds and lakes can also form. How? As a glacier moves, part of it breaks off. The ice chunk is buried under till. It forms a hole. The ice melts, and the hole fills with water. This is called a **kettle**. Labrador Pond in New York is an example.

Labrador
Pond

Aletsch Glacier

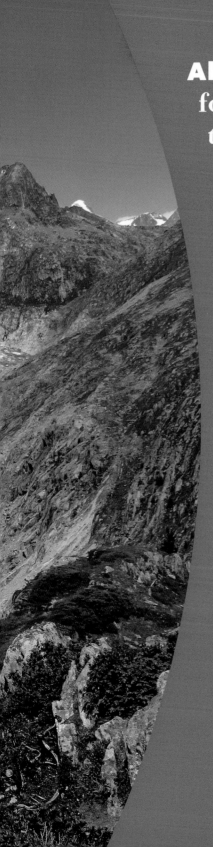

Alpine glaciers are glaciers that form high on mountains. Then they move down the mountain. They move through valleys and change them. Aletsch Glacier is one. It is in Switzerland.

Alpine glaciers form **glacial troughs**. These are U-shaped valleys. Their floors, or bottoms, are flat. The Glencoe pass in Scotland is one.

DID YOU KNOW?

Some glaciers made valleys along ocean shores. These filled with water. They are called **fjords**. We can see them in Norway.

Glencoe
pass

Matterhorn

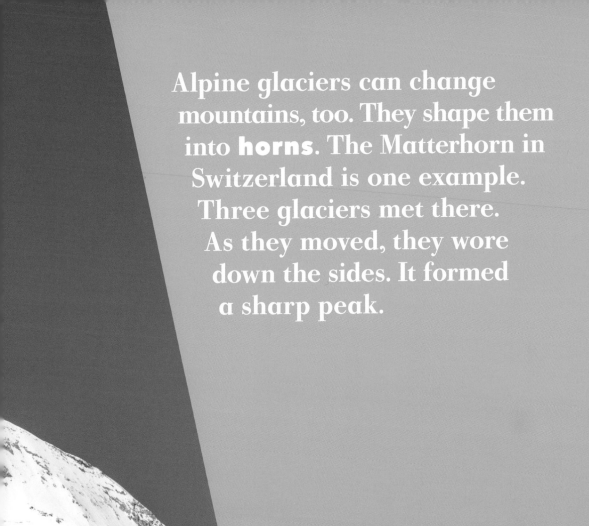

Alpine glaciers can change mountains, too. They shape them into **horns**. The Matterhorn in Switzerland is one example. Three glaciers met there. As they moved, they wore down the sides. It formed a sharp peak.

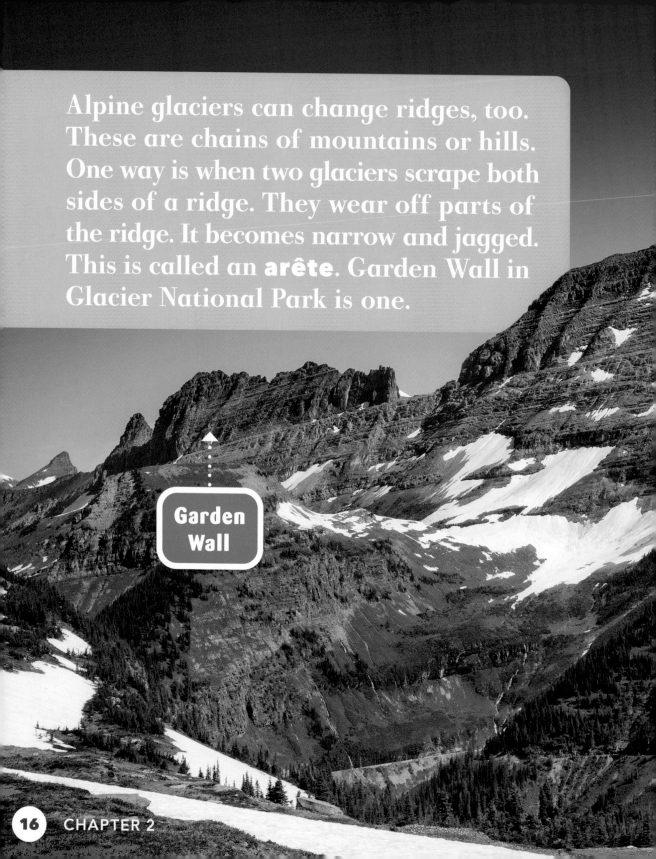

Alpine glaciers can change ridges, too. These are chains of mountains or hills. One way is when two glaciers scrape both sides of a ridge. They wear off parts of the ridge. It becomes narrow and jagged. This is called an **arête**. Garden Wall in Glacier National Park is one.

Garden
Wall

TAKE A LOOK!

How can alpine glaciers shape the land? Take a look!

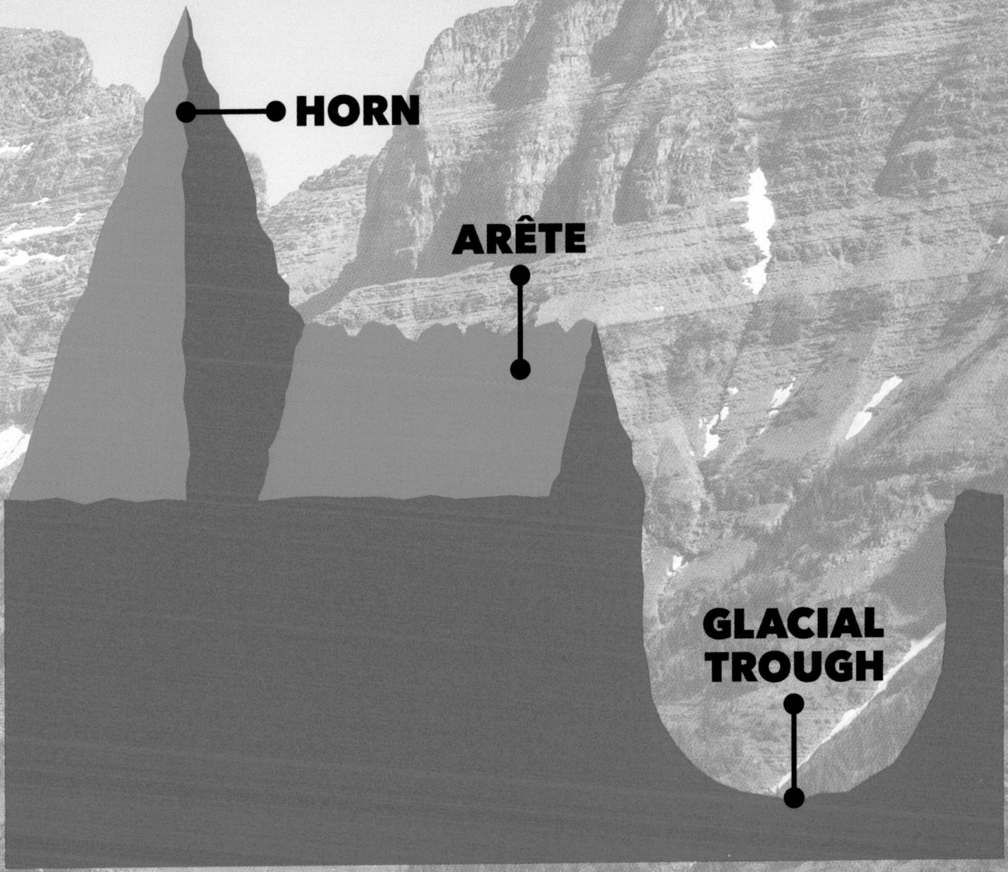

HORN

ARÊTE

GLACIAL TROUGH

CHAPTER 3

THE FUTURE OF GLACIERS

Glaciers melt and reshape as the **climate** changes. We see this today. **Global warming** is changing the planet. Glaciers are melting.

This change is hard for animals. Polar bears, penguins, and more live on ice. Their homes are shrinking. As glaciers melt, **sea levels** rise. Our planet continues to change.

Glaciers have changed much of Earth. We can help slow their melting. How? Work to save **energy**. Reduce waste. Reuse items. **Recycling** helps, too! How can you help care for Earth?

DID YOU KNOW?

About 70 percent of the fresh water on Earth is in glaciers! If all of the glaciers on land melted, the sea level would rise 230 feet (70 m). That is taller than six telephone poles!

ACTIVITIES & TOOLS

TRY THIS!

MAKE YOUR OWN GLACIER

Make your own glacier and see what happens as it melts and moves downhill!

What You Need:
- sand or dirt
- small plastic container
- water
- freezer
- flat tray or cookie sheet
- books

❶ Sprinkle sand or dirt into the bottom of the container. Fill the container with water and put it in the freezer.

❷ Once frozen, remove the ice chunk from the container. Place it on the tray or cookie sheet. Sprinkle more sand or dirt on top.

❸ Stack the books and lean one end of the tray or cookie sheet against it to make a slight ramp.

❹ Place your glacier at the top of the tray or cookie sheet. Let it go and observe what happens. How does it move? What is left behind?

GLOSSARY

alpine glaciers: Glaciers that form at the tops of mountains and move downward toward valleys.

arête: A sharp-crested ridge that is formed when two glaciers move past either side of a ridge.

climate: The weather typical of a place over a long period of time.

continental glaciers: Large, slow-moving masses of ice that cover very large areas.

energy: Usable power.

fjords: Long, narrow inlets of the ocean between high cliffs.

glacial troughs: Long, U-shaped valleys with steep sides and flat floors that were carved by glaciers.

global warming: An increase in Earth's average temperature.

gravity: The force that pulls things toward the center of Earth and keeps them from floating away.

horns: Pointed mountain peaks that are formed when glaciers erode a mountain into a sharp point.

icebergs: Large masses of ice floating in the ocean.

ice sheets: Permanent layers of ice that span a large area.

kettle: A depression that forms when a block of ice breaks off from a glacier, is buried, and slowly melts, leaving a pit.

recycling: Processing old items, such as glass, plastic, or newspapers, so they can be used to make new products.

sea levels: The average levels of the ocean's surface, used as starting points from which to measure the heights or depths of places.

till: Clay, sand, gravel, and boulders that are ground down and moved by glaciers.

INDEX

Aletsch Glacier 11

alpine glaciers 11, 12, 15, 16, 17

animals 19

arête 16, 17

continental glaciers 4

fjords 12

Garden Wall 16

glacial troughs 12, 17

Glencoe pass 12

global warming 18

gravity 6

Great Ice Age 4, 5

horns 15, 17

icebergs 6

ice sheets 5, 6

Jakobshavn Glacier 6

kettle 9

Labrador Pond 9

Matterhorn 15

mountains 11, 15, 16

ridges 16

sea levels 19, 20

till 8, 9

valleys 11, 12

TO LEARN MORE

Finding more information is as easy as 1, 2, 3.

❶ Go to www.factsurfer.com

❷ Enter "howglaciersshapedEarth" into the search box.

❸ Choose your book to see a list of websites.

FACT
SURFER